"Since I am one of the teachers in the movie and book "The Secret", and have been teaching the Law of Attraction for many years, I have also been recommending the emWave and the Inner Balance technologies to anyone who wants to more quickly create a 'vibrational match' for the things they want to attract into their life. Our emotions (joy, love, caring, compassion, appreciation) are the key, and many people do not know how to intentionally create the emotional states they want. The HeartMath tools and the emWave and Inner Balance technologies are ideal for easily and effortlessly accomplishing this."

Jack Canfield, Co-creator of the *Chicken Soup for the Soul*® series, Co-author of The Success *Principles*™, and

"The emWave or Inner Balance technology can take people quickly to where they try to get to through years of meditation."

John Gray, author Men are from *Mars, Women are from Venus*

"The emWave [or Inner Balance] technology is especially helpful to people who want to meditate but have little time; have been told by their doctor they need to meditate but don't know how; and for anyone who has been through the frustration of trying to meditate and having a hard time quieting their mind — now you can with this personal pocket meditation assistant that takes you there."

John Räätz, Founder & CEO of The Visioneering Group, whose clients have included Eckhart Tolle, What the Bleep Do We Know?!, Peaceful Warrior,

"I've been doing research on happiness for many years, and I'm thoroughly impressed with the Institute of HeartMath's products. HeartMath is on the leading edge of research and technology in the area of the heart's influence on health and happiness. I've found that their tools are powerful and effective in helping people raise their level of happiness. I love using the emWave and the Inner Balance technologies and the other

HeartMath Meditation Assistant

Integrating emWave® & Inner Balance™ Technologies

● ● ● ●

HeartMath tools to feel more open, centered, and joyful. I whole-heart-edly recommend them to everyone!"

Marci Shimoff, author of *Happy for No Reason*, co-author of the #1 NY Times best-sellers, *Chicken Soup for the Woman's Soul*, *Chicken Soup for the Mother's Soul*, and a featured teacher in the hit film, The Secret.

HeartMath Meditation Assistant

Integrating emWave & Inner Balance Technologies

Deborah Rozman, Ph. D.

HeartMath Meditation Assistant

Integrating emWave® & Inner Balance™ Technologies

● ● ● ●

2050-0807

HeartMath Meditation Assistant
Integrating emWave® & Inner Balance™ Technologies

●●●●

Welcome!

This **HeartMath Meditation Assistant** provides you with a comprehensive understanding of how to use the HeartMath heart coherence techniques and the emWave or the Inner Balance technology to enhance your spiritual/self-help practices. We suggest you read each section carefully to get a full understanding of the material and then you can easily refer back to the information that is most relevant to you and your specific interest and needs.

Here's an overview of what you will find in this guide.
Valuable information about:
- Meditation, prayer, mindfulness and other practices
- Common challenges to getting the most out of spiritual/self-help practices
- Why adding heart coherence to spiritual/self-help practices can enhance them
- How the heart coherence technology can help you increase the effectiveness of spiritual or personal growth practices

Instruction on:
- How to operate emWave or Inner Balance technology
- Instruction on how to practice the Quick Coherence® Technique
- How to use the emWave or Inner Balance technology with spiritual/self-growth practices
- Creating a new baseline of ease and intuitive connection
- Instruction on how to practice the Heart Lock-In® Technique
- Adding heart to increase personal and global coherence and the Global Coherence Initiative.

••••

Throughout, you will find interesting stories and testimonials from people who have used the HeartMath methods to assist their meditation or mindfulness practices and gain more inner peace, clarity and connection to to the intuitive guidance of their heart.

Enjoy!

Table of Contents

HeartMath Meditation Assistant

Integrating emWave® & Inner Balance™ Technologies

••••

● ● ● ●

HeartMath Meditation Assistant

As told in most cultures throughout human history, the key to restoring the harmony of body, mind, and community lies in the heart. It is not surprising that in the last few years more people than ever from different backgrounds and all walks of life are looking for a deeper heart connection.

With more heart, people want to increase discernment in decisions and in interactions with family, friends, and co-workers. They want to feel whole and well. In the search for wholeness, an improved quality of life and spiritual fulfillment, many people are using meditation, mindfulness, prayer and self-help practices.

A 2004 Center for Disease Control and Prevention survey found that 19 million people in the United States practice meditation. Millions more practice mindfulness, prayer, visualization or affirmation techniques. Until now, people have not had an easy way to see, scientifically, how their heart responds to these processes, and to use that information to find a deeper heart connection in their practices. Now you can.

HeartMath Meditation Assistant will help you develop that deeper heart connection, refine your practices, and get more value out of the time and energy you put into your efforts. The emWave or the Inner Balance (IBT) heart rhythm coherence technology both give instant feedback that shows you whether you are actually in a heart-centered and aligned state. It also, most importantly, guides you to get further into an optimal state to facilitate your practices.

HeartMath Meditation Assistant

Integrating emWave® & Inner Balance™ Technologies

●●●●

Using emWave or Inner Balance as a meditation assistant can be a facilitator to any system of meditation, prayer, self-help or healing techniques. In this program, all systems and techniques are honored and respected. Whatever practices you follow, using emWave or Inner Balance technology creates more ease and flow from the heart, which helps you get the most out of your meditations or affirmations and feel the benefits you are seeking more quickly. Follow this guide and you will learn how to use these devices to experience new enrichment from your practices.

Benefits many people hope to experience from meditation
•Stress Management • Reduced Anxiety • Inner Peace Lower Blood Pressure • Improved Health Improved Perception • Improved Ability to Focus More Intuitive Guidance and Discernment Deeper Compassion for Others • More Self-Control Increased Spiritual Awareness • More Heart Connection

---

●●●●

What Do You Really Want from Meditation?

People have different reasons for following meditative practices or other methods. Some want to relax and relieve stress. Others want to affirm or pray for positive changes they'd like to see manifest in their lives. Still others want to feel an inner alignment with something higher than themselves, receive intuitive answers to questions, develop inner knowledge, or help others or the world. To get started with this program, write down the three most important objectives or benefits that you want to gain from your practices.

1. _____
2. _____
3. _____

What Gets in the Way?

Perhaps, at times, you find that the benefits you seek from your practices are taking longer than you'd hoped or are harder to experience these days. Don't feel alone. Many people are experiencing this. There is a reason for it.

The increasing amount of stress and "busyness" in the world creates a type of static that can make it harder to get centered and stay focused. You invest 10 minutes, 20 minutes, or longer and hope to feel more peaceful or more inspired by the time you are done. However, very often, you can find that you are spending a good portion of your meditation time just trying to chill, calm down, and quiet the mind. You can find that your mind keeps drifting off planning your day, thinking about an upcoming conversation or turning over a problem. Or, you might find that

●●●●

you are falling asleep or daydreaming away your meditation time.

These factors create what we call "downtime" in meditation. This can leave you feeling frustrated, inadequate, worrying you "aren't doing it right" or "will never get there." Even people who have been meditating for years can find themselves spending more time musing about issues. They have some relative focus, but if they could honestly track what was going on, they might be surprised to see how much time is lost drifting. This is understandable. High speed changes are taking place in the world and everyone is adjusting to the accelerating rate. Sometimes it's harder for the mind and emotions to keep up with the pace, which can block heart flow and ease.

A long time practitioner of meditation and other self-help methods, HeartMath Institute founder and researcher, Doc Childre, understands how the stress environment is disrupting people's internal rhythms, making it harder to focus, quiet the mind and emotions, and stay centered in the heart. That's one reason he created the emWave and the Inner Balance technologies.

Doc commented, "These days people need to feel their heart and spirit more, to bring them peace, intuitive guidance, love and happiness. They want to take control of their life instead of having to just hang on because of the speed up of stress, with their emotions hanging in one place and their mind in another. People want to know they're investing their time in something that's effective and gives them an advantage. They need tools that help open the heart to create a portal for drawing in more spirit so they can find a more peaceful flow through the changing rhythms of life."

So, the next step in using this program to increase your effectiveness with meditation, mindfullness, prayer, visualization or other self-help methods is to identify what gets in your way.

Write down what gets in the way for you.

1. _____
2. _____
3. _____

What Can You Do About It?

In times of stress increase and fast-paced change, it's especially important to add more heart to your practices.

Many people are trying to meditate more from the heart these days. There's an intuitive knowing that the more sincere heart feeling you put into your meditation or other practice, the more effective it can be. When someone says, "put your heart into it" or "sing from the heart" or "go deep into your heart for the answer," they are saying to put more heart power and care into your intention. Adding more heartfelt energy helps you center and adds more ease and flow.

You can learn to center your heart intention—your heart's desire to feel more spiritual connection or to empower your efforts. Heart centering is like a gateway to facilitation from your spirit. It's a gateway to re-energize your system, because heart centering helps create mental, emotional and physical alignment or *coherence*.

Why HeartMath Can Help

The HeartMath techniques and technologies are designed to increase heart coherence, which is an alignment of your emotions, mind, body and spirit. Heart coherence is a distinct, synchronized mode of physiological functioning that is frequently associated with the experience of sustained positive emotion. The emWave or Inner Balance technology measures your heart rhythm, the beat-to-beat changes in your heart rate (known as heart rate variability).

Research has found that the pattern of your heart rhythm reflects the state of your emotions and nervous system dynamics. It reveals the interaction between your parasympathetic nervous system, which slows heart rate to help you relax, and your sympathetic nervous system, which speeds up heart rate. Both branches of your nervous system respond to your mental and emotional activity, even your subconscious feelings. So your heart rhythm reflects your inner state and sets the pace for your whole system.

Your heart and brain talk to each other and the pattern of your heart rhythm also reveals how coherent or incoherent this inter-action is. For example, when you are feeling tense, irritable, impatient, frustrated or anxious, your heart rhythm shifts into a disordered and incoherent pattern. Your heart signals incoherence to the brain, which inhibits your higher brain functions and triggers a stress response. You can't perceive as clearly and old emotional issues can start coming to the surface.

On the other hand, when you feel heart qualities like sincere appreciation, care, compassion or love, your heart rhythm shifts into a more harmonious and coherent pattern, reflecting the emotional balance you feel inside. Your heart sends coherent signals to the brain and the brain synchronizes to the heart's coherent rhythm. Heart coherence also triggers positive hormonal releases. This makes it easier to experience peace, positive feelings and a deeper meditative state.

"When we feel love and kindness toward others, it not only makes others feel loved and cared for, but it helps us also to develop inner happiness and peace." **The Dalai Lama**

Changing Heart Rhythms

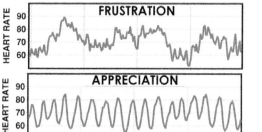

Getting in sync, which is reflected by heart rhythm coherence, powers up your ability to stay in the "now" and maintain presence or focused attention longer, bringing new perceptions and more intuitive discernment.

Heart rhythm coherence also enables you to self-regulate your autonomic nervous system, a goal of many yoga practices. The autonomic nervous system regulates over 90 percent of your body's internal functions, including hormonal and immune system responses, digestion, metabolism and sleep. Through heart rhythm coherence training on your emWave or Inner Balance device, you can learn to interact with and improve the functioning of your autonomic nervous system.

"We are a hospital leading in the practice of blending the best of alternative medicine with traditional medicine. It is our purpose to assist the patient to integrate their emotional life, their mental patterns, and their beliefs to support healing and health. We use the emWave or Inner Balance technology in our assessment of every patient. Using this tool, we establish a baseline for relative stress and relaxation for each individual. This information is helpful for all disciplines as we diagnose and support our patients toward healing. We also use this tool for basic meditation training with great results. This tool is foundational to our work restoring and enhancing patients' body-mind connection and the technology is robustly supported with research."

Jude Gladstone, Ph.D. Head, Psychology & Spiritual Programs, Sanoviv Medical Institute, Mexico

Using a simple HeartMath technique with your emWave or Inner Balance device at the start of or during meditation, prayer or other practices helps you center in the heart and activate heart rhythm coherence. Practicing heart coherence makes it progressively easier to experience sincere feelings of love, care, appreciation, gratitude, compassion, kindness and patience **at will.** With the technology as a meditation assistant, you connect more deeply with your heart to build a new **baseline of meditative coherence.**

A study of Zen monks found that the more advanced monks tended to have coherent heart rhythms. A study of long-term Buddhist practitioners found that while the practitioners generated a state of "unconditional loving-kindness and compassion," increases in gamma band oscillation and long-distance phase synchrony in the brain were also observed, which reflects a change in the quality of moment-to-moment awareness. The characteristic patterns of baseline activity in these long-term meditators were found to be different from those of a control group, suggesting that an individual's baseline state can be improved with practice. Another study of Buddhist monks using the same meditative focus of "loving-kindness and compassion" found an increase in heart rhythm coherence during this practice.

Tulku Thubten Rinpoche, a Tibetan Buddhist Dzogchen Master says,

"I find that practicing the HeartMath techniques is self-affirming, with a lot of value. It takes me to a place of very deep quality, deep peace. HeartMath gives pure method, without the need for belief. It can allow anyone to find enlightenment without having to follow a tradition. Many have that concept but no method. HeartMath offers a method. I doubt that there has ever been such on the planet before, or any institute like the Institute of HeartMath. The planet has evolved in intelligence to where people are ready for this now. It's about pure love. Buddhism teaches that. Pure love is the beginning and the end. In that state science and

awareness come together. You can be an agnostic, not believe in God even, and with HeartMath tools realize pure love and come to enlighten-ment or God. "

There are thousands of meditative practices. Most religions and spiritual disciplines teach some type of meditation or prayer to find peace and happiness within. In every major religion, love, appre-ciation, care and compassion are considered qualities of spirit that come from the heart—and it's important to note these are the same attitudes and feelings that generate heart rhythm coher-ence. Heart coherence feedback helps people realign their heart/ mind and emotions and develop their heart qualities— which gives them more access to their higher self and to intuitive discernment.

Whatever practices you do, using emWave or Inner Balance technology to stay in relative coherence during meditation can create more ease and flow at the start of or during your day. In fact, many meditators have found that 10 minutes meditating with heart coherence feedback to be more uplifting and effective than longer meditation sessions without that coherent alignment.

Adding Heart to Mindfulness Practices

The Dalai Lama exhorts us to, *"Develop the heart. Too much energy in your country is spent developing the mind instead of the heart. Develop the heart. Be compassionate. "*

Developing the heart strengthens and enriches the effectiveness of mindfulness practices. Many people experience HeartMath and Mindfulness as two complementary parts of the same wholeness intention to become more of their *true self.*

Mindfulness helps develop non-judgmental awareness, and as the study of Buddhist practitioners found, generating a state of unconditional loving-kindness and compassion increases the capacity and the quality of moment-to-moment awareness. HeartMath is helpful for developing the quality of your love and compassion, which bridges the connection to higher intelligence and guidance from your intuitive heart.

As Doc Childre HeartMath founder says, *"Mindful awareness is a forward moving practice for keeping our energetic conduits unblocked for the love, compassion and kindness that streams from our intelligent heart source."*

Health professionals and coaches often suggest that their clients practice mindfulness or observation meditations, where you learn to observe your thoughts and feelings without identifying with them. Using HeartMath technology to get into heart coherence first can help you stay centered from the observation place, so you don't get pulled as readily into identity with your thoughts and emotions. By staying in your heart center, you more easily let issues that come up just go by, without judging them good or bad or adding extra significance to them. Then your heart intuition may show you different attitudes or approaches to take. This is much different from the mind chewing over an issue trying to figure it out or emotionally processing the issue.

The emWave or Inner Balance technology will give you feedback in real-time if you start over-identifying with your thoughts or emotions. As your mind starts to wander or you start daydreaming, the audio tone and light (colored dot on the Inner Balance app) will change. This is your signal to shift back to a more genuine heartfelt state.

John Kabat-Zinn, a leading author and proponent of mindfulness writes, *"Awareness, like a field of com passionate intelligence located within your own heart, takes it all in and serves as a source of peace within the turmoil..."*

Below are stories from Mindfulness teachers on how they add HeartMath techniques and heart coherence technology to their own practice and training others.

"I have taught Mindfulness since the mid 90's to thousands of people. I now add how Heartmath goes hand in hand with Mindfulness practice with scientific data to back it up. I send all of my Mindfulness workshop participants to the HeartMath site to order the emWave or Inner Balance coherence technology. I tell them HeartMath coherence feedback is like "Mindfulness on Speed" and helps their Mindfulness practice. Since the mind always needs something to do, combining Mindfulness and

HeartMath Meditation Assistant
Integrating emWave® & Inner Balance™ Technologies

● ● ● ●

HeartMath helps me to meditate longer and have a richer, fuller experience. My mind is calmer integrating the two practices. I begin my Mindfulness sessions with the Body Scan. Next, I practice Mindfulness Breathing. Then I always finish my sessions with HeartMath techniques like Quick Coherence. The HeartMath technology helps me to practice Mindful Breathing. Meditators can easily get lost in their thoughts for a length of time before realizing they have strayed, and feel their mind has hijacked their practice. The Inner Balance or the emWave technology instantly detects and shows me when my mind wanders from mindfully following my breath. "

Janet (Alston) Jackson – HeartMath Certified Coach/Mentor; Mindfulness Teacher/ Speaker and USA Book News Award-Winning Author

"Yesterday I used my emWave during my break at a full day workshop on Mindful Stress Management for mental health professionals. The audience consisted of practicing mental health, educational and medical professionals and the workshop was sponsored by a local hospital. The primary goal of the workshop was to help mental health professionals/ educators integrate meditation into their work. The secondary goal was to help the mental professionals cope with the stress that can come from helping others. In fact, that workshop even used the terms gaining an 'inherent sense of coherence." For me, emWave is a perfect way to engage my meditation autopilot, shifting from fight or flight to FLOW without distracting, internal verbal chatter. The emWave helps me effortlessly shift my attention to where it needs to be (kind of like a compass). I would recommend the emWave to both the beginner and the professional. It is a great educational tool to aid in establishing good stress management and meditation (which normally takes about 8 weeks with guided practice). It can serve as the "training-wheels" to achieve a sense of balance until one knows what a balanced state feels like AND how to bring about the sense of balance at will."

Dr. Ron Rubenzer - author of How the Best Handle Stress

HeartMath Meditation Assistant

Integrating emWave® & Inner Balance™ Technologies

●●●●

"My clients have reported that HeartMath coherent breathing is very grounding and usually "lands" them in present time, with an attitude of open awareness. They also realized that just "regulating" your breathing by counting would not sustain a state of coherence. This requires the ability to elicit and sustain a feeling of appreciation. As a Mindfulness instructor this is my "IN" to the concept of observing what is, without judgment, while remaining connected to the body through coherent breathing. By making the invisible (regulation of the autonomic nervous system) visible (using any of the HeartMath devices), clients understand faster that mindfulness is the art of having your "mind and feet in the same place".

Pilar Angel, CCHT certified, 2015 MBSR Foundational Teacher Training at UCSD, Heartmath® Certified Coach/Mentor

"For years I practiced meditation techniques stemming from basic mindfulness and Zen Buddhism before coming across HeartMath. Mindfulness is a wonderful concentration technique, but without structured focus can leave me wallowing in negative mind states. I have found that adding HeartMath coherence technology and HeartMath techniques to my mindfulness practice ensures that I am able to shift quickly into a positive (or 'coherent') emotional state, benefiting my body, mind and soul. I make better use of my sitting meditation time. I move more quickly into a space of heart-based appreciation and this helps me to release stress and unhelpful emotional knots that I have been holding onto. It also resets my system allowing me to flow more during the rest of my day (or to sleep better at night). Over time, I have become much more able to find that place of coherence (or inner balance) with just a few breaths while on the move."

Will Stephens - Lead Mindfulness Teacher Trainer, Youth Mindfulness (UK).

• • • •

"I've experimented with various forms of mindfulness meditation over the course of many years. Like many people, I struggled with quieting my thoughts. On more than one occasion, I gave up and assumed that traditional meditation just wasn't for me because I wasn't noticing enough productive results from my efforts. Then I discovered HeartMath, and when I added heart coherence to my practice, it changed my life. For me, heart awareness was the missing piece of the mindfulness puzzle. The art of focusing on my heart, instead of my thoughts, helped me step beyond mental busyness to explore deeper realms of awareness within my mind, body, emotions, and intuition.

HeartMath's extensive scientific research persuaded the skeptical part of my mind there was indeed extraordinary value in this practice. Now, my mindfulness meditation practice includes being present with my heart, my feelings, my senses and my values. Meanwhile, that busy analytical part of my mind can relax because it has learned that activating an inner state of appreciation creates order and harmony throughout my system (and the flow of anti-aging hormones is a nice bonus!). The practice of connecting with my heart has yielded insights that I couldn't have reached through my intellect alone.

HeartMath's emphasis on emotional awareness is a perfect adjunct to our Mindful Eating coursework. Teaching Mindfulness is a subtle art that is inherently subjective in nature. We reference HeartMath's research because it provides evidence-based data on the physiological benefits of awareness practices, along with effective methods to measure and monitor results. As students see the illustrations that show the visual differences between chaotic and coherent heart rate variability patterns, they can quickly recognize how their thoughts and emotions directly influence their physiology. Using the Inner Balance app and getting real-time feedback makes the process more tangible. The HeartMath techniques are easy for people to learn and can be seamlessly integrated with modern lifestyles. What's missing in many people's lives is a sense of meaning, purpose and fulfilment. The HeartMath techniques encourage participants to actively cultivate qualities of the heart, including appreciation, gratitude and care. A regular mindfulness practice that includes heart coherence enhances physical, mental, emotional and overall wellbeing."

Lauren Archer - Mindfulness Program Director, Sound Medical Weight Loss

"I combine HeartMath techniques with practices of focused awareness in my toolkit of mindfulness for my private and corporate clients. The two practices are symbiotic in my experience as they deepen one's capacity to develop more attuned situational awareness to both whole body experiences that manifest as stress and anxiety as well as the ensuing incoherent states that occur when the sympathetic nervous system kicks into high gear. I find that my HeartMath training that is specific to coherence and heart rate variability offer deep understanding of human physiology and dovetail perfectly with the practices of learning to sustain and focus attention that are key to mindfulness. I hold this as living wholeheartedly and mindfully — an awakened way to consciously experience being human."

Suzanne Jewell, Chief Mindfulness Officer, World Happiness Summit, HeartMath®
Certified Business Coach

"I've used heart coherence technology with my clients and in my personal practice and have found that coherence leads to a more settled meditation practice. I've also noticed that when my meditation practice is highly heart coherent, I experience fuller and more positive experiences in my daily life. I've enjoyed working with leaders in many industries over the years. Those that touched me and led spirited organizations shared a mindful presence that was palpable. What I came to learn from them was that being mindful is the first step in being fully present. But what truly

set these leaders apart was their heartfulness and embodied sense of courage to act in the direction of what matters most. Something magical happens when meeting someone who lives in a coherent state of mind, body, soul, and mission."

Peter Baverso – HeartMath® Certified Trainer for the US Marine Corps, Justice Department, Veterans and Leadership teams.

"Using HeartMath technology with teenagers with behavioural and attentional challenges has been transformative to their experience of mindfulness meditation. I saw them experience a real sense of mastery and an engagement with the practice that allowed them to, perhaps for the first time, really connect with their hearts. HeartMath technology became something they continually sought to return to."

Dr Lyndsay Lunan- Mindfulness Teacher, Youth Mindfulness, UK. Psychology Lecturer, City of Glasgow College, UK.

"I observe the seamless interface and interaction of Mindfulness practices and HeartMath tools/techniques every day in my clinical practice. I see this across the lifespan with children, teens and adults, as I coach them in developing self-regulations skills. I use HeartMath and mindfulness practices in intensive day treatment, inpatient and outpatient clinic settings, and as part of group training experiences.

Although many clients will understand the benefits of mindfulness, they may find the initial experience of and subsequent practice of mindfulness as being vague/mysterious and are uncertain as to whether they are doing it effectively or correctly. HeartMath can take the guesswork out of it. HeartMath technologies, such as Inner Balance, provide clear, compelling evidence for the mind-body connection. Clients/patients can observe in real-time that as they engage in mindfulness techniques of all kinds, there is a corresponding change in physiological response patterns as reflected in their heart rhythms. This is exciting and validating for clients.

HeartMath Meditation Assistant

Integrating emWave® & Inner Balance™ Technologies

●●●●

Mindfulness practices are inherently flexible and can take many forms. Mindfulness and HeartMath are each about "awareness", self-regulation of emotions and attention, and being "in the moment" in their own way. HeartMath tools/technologies can enhance the ability to initiate mindful states and experiences, and bring a sense of "objectivity" to the process that is very helpful for many. For day-to-day practice, adults and kids need something compelling and interactive to engage their interest and convince them to continue to invest time and energy integrating self-regulation into their busy lives. HeartMath is the answer! HeartMath techniques and technologies evoke curiosity, and provide a user-friendly structure for making the practice of emotional regulation, stress management and mindful practices much more fun! I tell kids and teens that the HeartMath approach is like "technology-assisted meditation."

For those who might struggle with the effective, structured practice of mindfulness strategies, learning Heartmath skills, such as the Quick Coherence technique, naturally initiate a "shift" that can then quiet down the mind and body and allow for a natural, easy transition to mindfulness activities. With kids and teens who are commonly on high "arousal", HeartMath (emWave or Inner technology and techniques) can provide new transitional activities/opportunities to assist them into desired mindful states and therapeutic interventions.

Mindfulness and heart coherence techniques/technologies are mutually reinforcing. In mindfulness, we become immersed in the moment, non-judgmentally, without distraction, engaging all of our senses. One outcome of this is to be better able to tolerate and regulate intense emotions without avoidance. HeartMath technologies are all about emotional regulation, building on and intensifying mindfulness elements in a multisensory

way, engaging tactile, auditory, and visual experiential elements that can deepen the experience of mindful awareness. When we initiate the coherent state utilizing HeartMath techniques, we are facilitating enhanced cognitive function and clarity of mind, which in turn reinforces the mindfulness state and experience, as we quiet the mind and body. "

Timothy Culbert, MD, FAAP, Developmental/Behavioral Pediatrician; Medical Director: Integrative Medicine PrairieCare Medical Group; Co-Founder of Natural Mental Health Online; HeartMath Interventions Instructor

Using HeartMath Technology with Prayer

Most of the world's religions use prayer as an important and essential spiritual practice and prayer takes on many forms. Below are stories from people of different faiths sharing how they use emWave or Inner Balance technology to enhance prayer.

Christian—The New Testament

"A good man out of the good treasure of his heart bringeth forth that which is good" Luke, chapter 6, verse 45

Bonnie St. John, Olympic Medalist, author of *How Strong Women Pray*, and a speaker named by NBC as one of the five most inspiring women in the nation, describes her experience using emWave technology with prayer:

"Prayer is my conversation with God. Sometimes, it feels like there is static on the line coming from my own states of discontent, stress, fear, and confusion. To reduce the static and feel the presence of God more closely, we have always been taught to be in gratitude, be still, and feel love, like the techniques in the HeartMath system help you do. I find that the HeartMath tools provide an interesting set of structures and steps to help me go deeper into prayer more easily and to eliminate the static——a process that can be confusing and bewildering. The emWave or Inner Balance technology helps by providing a way of really seeing what you are doing and has helped me pray more deeply. At first I thought measuring my vital signs while praying was a pretty crazy idea. But when you understand the research about how this technology measures a peaceful state in physiological terms, it makes a lot of sense. Getting coherent using the HeartMath system makes my prayer time more rewarding, more true, more connected, more sincere."

Jewish—The Old Testament

"For as a man thinketh in his heart, so is he" Proverbs, chapter 23, verse 7

"There is a Hasidic saying, 'Everyone should carefully observe which way his heart draws him and then choose that way with all his strength.' The emWave technology helps to motivate me. I use emWave 6 mornings a week, religiously, before I go to pray at a Yeshiva. I feel that emWave helps me to negotiate with myself. It helps me to pull myself together, and become calm and motivated to walk out to pray early each morning. I do some exercises and then finish off with the emWave for two or three cycles of the full scale count. This prepares me for the prayer session which lasts about 20 minutes or so. I make the emWave a prerequisite each morning, without fail."   **Harry Pearle**

Qur'an

"God will not call you to account for thoughtlessness in your oaths, but for the intention in your hearts" 002.225

"I have been using the emWave for several months. I find it very grounding and calming. As a practicing Muslim who prays five times a day, my experience is that I cut out the cares of the world and tune in quicker when I use the emWave. Also I am generally a calmer, happier person.

Mohammed Shafiq, Asian Health Advisor

Hindu— Chandogya Upanishad

"There is a light that shines beyond all things on earth, beyond the highest, the very highest heavens. This is the light that shines in your heart." (3.13.7)

HeartMath Meditation Assistant

Integrating emWave® & Inner Balance™ Technologies

● ● ● ●

"I am an 82 year old practicing Hindu in the UK. I lost my husband 18 months ago. Luckily I came across HeartMath last year and use the emWave when possible. In 6 months time my high blood pressure (which I've had for 35 years) dropped to the extent that I have stopped all my drugs and my sense of smell has partially returned. Every Sunday I attend the Hindu Temple and have noticed since using the emWave my focus is better and my prayers mean more."

Mrs. Sushila Sinha, MA Psych., author of 'Developmental Psychology'

Sikh—(derived from Hinduism)

"I had been very stressed for the last 5 years. I took over the Post Office 18 months ago and found life even more strenuous. My doctor advised me to use emWave technology and I have done so for the last 6 months. Now I manage the Post Office without even a thought and am loving my work and my home life again. Being a practicing Sikh I was astonished that even my prayers are better. I go deeper into myself. Thank you HeartMath.

Vazir Singh, Postmaster

Buddhist - The Dhammapada (a collection of the oral teachings of the Buddha)

"The way is not in the sky. The way is in the heart." (18:255)

"I use the emWave in my daily morning sitting meditation. It's a Soto Zen (Buddhist) meditation (zazen). The focus is a state called 'shikantaza' (just sitting) which means one puts the cognitive mind on hold. This could be expressed as 'Just sit, don't know mind, ' and getting in the green on the emWave helps you do this, and maintaining this state will keep you in the green. "

Marty Slater, Oriental Healing Arts

●●●●

Heart-Power Your Intentions and Affirmations

You can also use your heart rhythm coherence technology to add power to your intentions, visualizations and affirmations. The heart is the power behind higher manifestation. As you practice activating the coherent power of your heart, it brings heart, mind and body into alignment to draw the highest best to you. This coherent alignment draws in more of your spirit and higher discernment faculties—your intuition—to help facilitate the manifestation of deeper heart-felt intentions in all aspects of your life.

You can't use emWave or Inner Balance technology for negative intention, as that generates incoherence between the mind and heart. You can't cheat or fool yourself with the technology. It keeps you honest with yourself. You're either in coherence or you're not. But you can use it to help clear negative emotional patterns and self-doubt that take away from your affirmations. Practice of heart coherence helps to clear old negative patterning stored in the cells, releasing more power for creative intention and manifestation from your true self. Practicing heart coherence can especially help you make positive changes in areas you thought you couldn't, while having more peace and acceptance with issues you can't change.

If your practices include affirmations or visualizations, take a moment to write down three heartfelt intentions that you want to manifest.

1. _____

2. _____

3. _____

HeartMath Meditation Assistant
Integrating emWave® & Inner Balance™ Technologies

●●●●

While using the emWave or Inner Balance technology, set your intention and align your heart (feeling) with your visualization or affirmation (thought) to create the highest outcome, what's highest best for all concerned. There's a difference between heart-infused intention and mind-willpower intention. As heart is added to intention, it aligns you more with the power of your spirit. Learning to sustain high coherence on your emWave or Inner Balance device for longer periods will draw in more of your spirit to strengthen your aim to follow through on your heart-infused intentions and commitments.

"I want to highly recommend the tools and techniques of HeartMath. I, my staff, and my family have been using the HeartMath techniques and the emWave or Inner Balance technology device with great success— both to create more stress-free states of being and also to make more heart-coherent decisions. Since I am one of the teachers in the movie and book The Secret, and have been teaching the Law of Attraction for many years, I have also been recommending the emWave or Inner Balance to anyone who wants to more quickly create a 'vibrational match' for the things they want to attract into their life. Our emotions (joy, love, caring, compassion, appreciation) are the key, and many people do not know how to intentionally create the emotional states they want. The HeartMath tools, the emWave and Inner Balance technologies are ideal for easily and effortlessly accomplishing this.

Jack Canfield, Co-creator of the *Chicken Soup for the* Soul® series, Co-author of *The Success Principles*™

• • • •

Getting Started with emWave or Inner Balance technology

Step 1—Learn to Operate your emWave or Inner Balance device

To get the most from this program, you'll need to become familiar with how to operate this heart rhythm coherence technology which has earned the Seal of Approval and Award for Distinction and Innovation from the American Institute of Stress. This technology has been developed from over two decades of scientific research on the heart, brain and nervous system, conducted by Doc Childre and HeartMath Institute.

- Remove the contents from the box and follow the installation instructions.
- Review the Quick Start Guide or Owner's Manual and get to know the features.
- Visit this site for more helpful training: https://www.heartmath. com/heartmath-technology-free-training/
- If you have the Inner Balance technology, download the free app from your app store.
- Watch the two short Tutorial Videos: HeartMath Introduction and Inner Balance Introduction. If they don't play automatically when you first start your app, go to: Settings / Tutorials.
- If you have the emWave2, download the software into your computer.

Step 2—Learn the Quick Coherence® Technique

The Quick Coherence Technique is designed to bring your heart rhythms into coherence quickly. With the technique, you will generate a heart-focused, positive emotional state, so that coherence emerges naturally and is easy to sustain. The Quick Coherence

● ● ● ●

Technique is not a replacement for your meditative practice, but helps you create a new baseline of coherence for improved results. So it's important to learn this simple technique, which you can do in several ways:

Practice the simple steps outlined on the next page.

If you have the emWave2, connect it to your computer, click on Games/Visualizers then click on Coherence Coach® for guided instructions. If you have the emWave Desktop or emWave Pro, click on the Coherence Coach tab. If you have the Inner Balance trainer app, the Tutorial Audio should start to play once you open your app. If not, go to Settings / Tutorials / Tutorial Audio in Settings.

Quick Coherence Technique

Step 1: Focus your attention in the area of the heart. Imagine your breath is flowing in and out of your heart or chest area, breathing a little slower and deeper than usual.

Suggestion: Inhale 5 seconds, exhale 5 seconds (or whatever rhythm is comfortable).

Putting your attention around the heart area helps you center and get coherent.

Step 2: Make a sincere attempt to experience a regenerative feeling such as appreciation or care for someone or something in your life.

Suggestion: Try to re-experience the feeling you have for someone you love, a pet, a special place, an accomplishment, etc., or focus on a feeling of calm or ease.

Step 3—Practice the Quick Coherence Technique while using your emWave or Inner Balance unit

- Once you've learned the Quick Coherence Technique, you're ready to practice it with heart coherence feedback. Your goal is to get the light at the top of your emWave2 (or color on your

●●●●

Inner Balance app) to turn from red (low coherence) which is normal, to blue (medium coherence) which is much improved, to green (high coherence) the optimal state.

Most meditation practices start with centering and some form of breathing exercise to help calm the mind and emotions and find an inner stillness. From that centered place, you become more mindful of your feelings and thoughts and have more ability to sustain your meditative intentions. Heart-Focused Treathing activates the power of your heart, and activating a calm or regenerative feeling, such as appreciation or sincere care, helps you stay in heart rhythm coherence. Staying in relative coherence during meditation will increase your power to access enriching heart feelings and maintain positive feelings during and after meditation. And who wouldn't want that?*

- Now practice the Quick Coherence technique with your emWave or Inner Balance technology and watch the light (or color) change from red to blue to green. Sustain blue or green as much as you can without trying too hard. Find a breathing rhythm that is natural and comfortable for you while you continue to feel a genuine positive emotion. Make it a gentle process.

Doc Childre's view is that:
"Using the emWave or Inner Balance technology takes the economy of meditation to such a new level, because of the instant feedback and realignment it gives you, resulting in increased

---

If you have an irregular heartbeat or arrhythmia, coherence practice may help. You may not be able to sustain heart rhythm coherence for long periods, but you can coherently align coherent heart qualities, mind, and emotions and feel the benefits.

effectiveness in shorter periods of time. People really need that now because of the increased pace of the world and all the things they have to do and the time crunches they have. The technology clinically gives you way more economy in the meditation process. You get a lot more for doing less, and we all need that these days. It literally gives you 'more bang for the buck' in a shorter period of time and you're still the one doing it. It's not the machine doing it, but what a coaching buddy it is."

Step 4—Use emWave or Inner Balance technology to build a new Baseline of Meditative Coherence

There are several ways you can use your emWave or Inner Balance to improve your meditative practice.

a. Practice the Quick Coherence Technique with the emWave or Inner Balance app at the start of your practice to center yourself in the heart and get aligned. Just spend five minutes increasing your coherence level before you start your meditation, prayer, visualization, affirmations or other practice.

b. Depending on the type of meditation you do, you may want to use emWave or Inner Balance while you are meditating. You can check the emWave or Inner Balance periodically to monitor your coherence level in your process. Whether you do 10 minute, 20 minute or 2 hour or longer meditations, the emWave or Inner Balance feedback can help you stay focused, especially when thoughts or mind rambling take over, and regain a deeper connectedness to your practice.

c. During meditation, you can turn on the audio tones if you want to keep your eyes closed. Listen to the changing audio tones to guide you into coherence.

●●●●

One tone indicates you are in medium coherence (blue) and another tone lets you know you are in high coherence (green). You can adjust the volume to low, medium, high or mute.

See if you can increase your amount of coherence over time (percent of time) in blue or green, average coherence or coherence achievement score. Increasing coherence helps build a stronger alignment between emotions, mind, body and spirit, enhancing the quality of your meditative practice. As your coherence ratio improves, you will be establishing a new baseline of meditative coherence.

emWave or Inner Balance technology Benefits

- Helps build a bridge between heart, mind and body that strengthens your spiritual connection, so more spirit can come into your heart

- Helps you find the state you hoped for—or get back to that state more quickly—and sustain meditation benefits longer

- Helps you stay grounded after meditating and get the most out of your time

d. During prayer, visualizations or affirmations, keep re-focusing in your heart while using the emWave or Inner Balance technology to build your ability to sustain heart powered intention. Use the Quick Coherence Technique and focus on radiating rings of positive feelings from the heart as you visualize or affirm your intention. As you imagine or think about what you're visualizing or affirming, your mind is more active and the coherence light (or color) may turn red. That's fine. When you're ready, simply focus back to the heart and keep recommitting to the feeling of your heart intention while sitting in medium or high coherence for five minutes or more.*

We all go through different energetic rhythms during a week or a month. There will be times when it can be harder to sustain the coherence level you achieved before or harder to maintain positive feelings and focus. Don't worry when this happens. Just staying in as much coherence as you can will help establish a more balanced rhythm between your mind, heart and emotions. This will develop intuitive guidance and sober discernment and compassion for self and others during those times. You'll feel more in charge of yourself.*

Remember that success isn't about driving the emWave or Inner Balance technology "into the green" through breathing; it's about seeing what thoughts and feelings take you in and out of your heart-centered state. With practice, you will identify new internal reference points of coherent heart feelings that you automatically calibrate back to during the day. This will help you build your new baseline of meditative coherence.

The Challenge Levels

The technology is factory set to challenge level 1. You can learn a lot about how thoughts and feelings affect your coherence

---

*Note: Once you make an internal shift, it can take from 1 to 10 seconds for the color to change, depending on where you are in the red, blue or green color threshold. If you find you aren't able to shift back into coherence easily, using the breath pacer can help you re-enter the coherence state. However, it takes feeling genuine heartfelt attitudes to sustain coherence. The emWave2 breath pacer is "smart" in that once you get into medium coherence (blue light), the pacer will adjust its speed to help you stay in coherence. The Inner Balance app coach is also smart, and scrolls coaching prompts along the bottom of the screen to help you stay in coherence. Sometimes meditators go into very shallow breathing, depending on the type of meditation they do. If this is your tendency, just breathe a little more deeply while you are meditating or try to find an even deeper feeling of genuine appreciation, gratitude, love or care and you'll move into higher coherence more easily.

at challenge level 1. Some people like to practice more refined states of focus and stillness at the higher challenge levels. Mental, emotional and physical rhythms can vary at times. Don't worry if you find at times that it's harder to stay in "the green" at a higher challenge level. When that occurs, just go back to a lower challenge level to stay in the green. Be assured, practicing at challenge level 1 is always effective and will increase your baseline of meditative coherence.

An emWave or Inner Balance Practice Plan

Practice increasing coherence on the emWave or Inner Balance for 5 minutes or longer at challenge level 1. Follow the Practice Plan suggested that comes with the device. As it gets easier for you to stay in high coherence (green) at challenge level 1 for long periods, you can move to challenge level 2.

Each challenge level will refine your skill at entering and sustaining medium or high coherence. After you get skilled at sustaining coherence at one level, you can move to the next level to sharpen your awareness and meditative skills. You may find that you have different inner experiences at the different challenge levels. It's not competitive. It's a fun exploration—between you and yourself.

"I am a practicing physician who is also a consistent meditator. I have used various meditation techniques over the years and, aside from 1-2 weeks total, I have meditated at least once and often twice a day every day for the past 32 years. I used the emWave Desktop before getting the mobile emWave. I bought the mobile emWave2 for my personal use as soon as it came out, because even with all the meditation, I have struggled to control my impatience and anger during the day. Getting into the

green at challenge level 1 and 2 during my meditations was easy, but the only way I found to get into the green consistently at level 3 is with heart and compassion-related breathing. Doing that has deepened my meditation and helped me stay calm while waiting for appointments, less anxious when seeing difficult patients and more able to listen from the heart in personal conflict situations. Now I use the emWave three times a day and instruct my patients to do the same. Thanks so much for the user-friendly little emWave. "

Diana Little, MD, MS, Ann Arbor MI

"When man is serene, the pulse of the heart flows and connects, just as pearls are joined together or like a string of red jade, then one can talk about a healthy heart."

The Yellow Emperor's Canon of Internal Medicine, 2500 B.C.

Heart-Based Living—Building a New Baseline of Coherencé

It's important to understand that what you do in your day has a direct impact on the quality and effectiveness of your meditative practices. When you move from meditation into day-to-day activity, your heart rhythms adjust according to the need. However, you'll have a **carryover** effect that accrues from your emWave or Inner Balance practice sessions which helps to increase clarity and intuitive discernment as you weigh your choices and make decisions.

The practice of building a new baseline of coherence leaves you more heart-centered and spirit-connected in day-to-day activities and interactions with others. This makes it easier for you to find the flow during the day or create flow where there is resistance. Using emWave or Inner Balance technology will help you reboot or reset your system after taxing energy expenditures, such as work overload, time pressures, long meetings, difficult people—the basic list.

The pace of life on the planet is speeding up and as a result people are experiencing more time deprivation and overwhelm— too much to do and not enough time to do it all. This requires another level of prioritizing what's important to you. The *carryover* effect from practicing coherence makes it easier to operate from your heart's intelligence and intuition and shift back into balance when you get out of the heart. A coherent alignment between heart, mind and emotions can lead to a new way of perceiving, thinking and relating which we call *heart-based living*. With genuine practice, we can find within our heart the answers and directions for the next steps along our path to becoming our empowered, true self.

●●●●

Here are two additional ways to integrate the emWave or
Inner Balance technology to help you build a new baseline of
coherence.

Doing 1-3 Minute On-the-Spot Meditations

Do 1-3 minute on-the-spot meditations with emWave or Inner
Balance technology when stressors step up during the day or at
times of the day when your energy drops. The emWave or Inner
Balance will give you an honest read-out to show you where you
really are and when you've shifted back into heart coherence.
It will help stabilize your emotions and cushion any reactions that
may come up.

Doing these on-the-spot meditations with emWave or Inner
Balance technology several times a day also helps release accumulated mental or emotional stress, boosting your "presence" and
vitality as you move through the next part of your day. Even long-
time meditators can find benefit from rebooting or resetting their
rhythms at challenge level 1 or 2 with 1-3 minute on-the-spot heart
coherence meditations. This will help raise your vibration and your
overall baseline meditative coherence.

"Prep" for Challenging Situations

Instead of worrying about what "might happen" during your day, you can stop a lot of energy drain by using the Quick Coherence Technique with or without the technology to lift your vibration and listen to voice of the heart for intuitive guidance before potentially stressful situations. This will help you get to neutral, a state where energy-draining perceptions like anxiety or judgments can shift. Go through the steps of Quick Coherence Technique with the heart intention of holding attitudes like non-judgment, calm, care, kindness or appreciation before you go into situations you know are likely to cause reactions and take you off your center. This is what we mean by prep. A tremendous amount of personal energy can be saved by prepping your attitudes with heart-based qualities and behaviors before engaging in situations. Care enough to go to your heart to get peace, clarity and direction before you act.

For example, say you tend to react to a co-worker. You can prep for an upcoming interaction by getting into heart coherence for a minute or two before you begin the conversation. You will be better able to handle any reaction, without sacrificing your intention to stay heart-centered and balanced.

It's also helpful to prep by getting into heart coherence before meetings or creative projects to increase your intuitive discernment abilities in those situations. It will especially help you listen and communicate from the heart, which can save a lot of time and energy and prevent a lot of stress.

The more you can reconnect heart qualities and attitudes, such as appreciation, kindness, care and compassion during the day, getting "in the green" with your emWave or Inner Balance tech-nology when possible, the more your body's glands and organs can work together with greater synchronization and harmony.

Progressively, you will experience an increase in energy, enthusi-asm and well-being. Things that usually bother you won't matter as much. Decisions, priorities, and solutions will become clearer. You'll have more access to your heart's intuitive guidance while weighing choices and decisions. It will be easier to be your genu-ine self in social situations. As you build your ability to sustain pos-itive feeling states and attitudes longer and shift back into them more quickly during your day, you boost your meditative progress. You will notice improvements that carry over into your morning or evening meditations.

"Using the emWave in the midst of all the 'busyness' of my work day, as well as before my meditation and visualization practices, has created some powerful insights. Most importantly I am getting on a deeper level how powerful it is to be detached from HOW I am going to accomplish things. The emWave has shown me that I am most coherent when I am BEING who I want to be and I am far from coherent when I am in the mode of 'trying to figure it out."

Robert MacPhee, Founder and President of Heart Set, Inc.

Your Heart's Intuitive Guidance

Coherence practice will give you a growing sense that you have a higher capacity and you are capable of higher and more effective choices in life. It does this by slowing down the mind and emotions so your heart's intuitive guidance can weigh in on your assessments and decisions. It increases your capacity to experience positive feelings like love, patience, kindness, appreciation, care, compassion, inner peace and forgiveness which deepen your connection to your heart's intuitive guidance. More people are realizing that it's a lack of coherent alignment that clouds the connection with their higher-capacity resources— such as their heart's intuition, care and empowerment, along with their soul's wisdom accumulated from all of their experiences.

"The beauty of the emWave or Inner Balance technology is that you can't fool it (and by extension yourself). You're either connected to the larger universal agenda or you're not. It's hard to have a personal agenda for long when in true coherence. The energy of coherence is the energy of benevolence towards others. With the emWave or Inner Balance, meditators can gain what hours of practice hasn't taught them about releasing personal agendas and getting to a unified understanding. People are so time-starved they need this to help them link in with the ever-present feasibility of coherence."

Jeddah Mali, Spiritual Mentor, Teacher and Consultant

Helping the Planet

Many people are asking what they can do to help the planet. You can help yourself, others and the world (and increase your sense of security) by radiating heart coherence, love, appreciation, care or compassion to people or to the planet in your meditations. This will become more important as the planetary consciousness shift unfolds.

Time and events are speeding up, but so is consciousness. The heart is a major portal to spirit and your higher self. Deeper gratitude, peace and security increase with spirit alignment. Practicing with emWave or Inner Balance heart coherence technology helps open the heart so you can experience more of your spirit's intuitive guidance through life's decisions. Holly explains how this happened for her:

"I searched out many paths of spirituality, oftentimes feeling like I was going through the motions of someone else's ritual. I realized upon discovering the emWave, that the element that was missing was a direct and palpable communication with a living force within me, my own heart. I had everyone else's input on what to do for spiritual growth and how to do it, and yet often my own heart's input was not actively a part of this process. Once I began to experience that by using the HeartMath techniques with the emWave technology, I found an internal voice of intuitive reason to guide me in this journey, and I made profound progress in learning to define my own spiritual direction and truth. The emWave technology is truly a miracle for humanity on a path to enlightenment. We must learn to bring ourselves, our own heart and our communication with the Divine, however it expresses itself within us, to our spiritual seeking if we are to ever truly unfold the purpose of our lives. "

Holly Thomas, Wellness Coach

●●●●

Help Build a Baseline of Social and Global Coherence

People have used meditation or prayer for thousands of years to send good thoughts and feelings of loving kindness, care and healing to others. But sometimes, those good intentions can turn into worry and anxiety. When you are worrying about someone you care about, for example, someone who is sick or who has relationship or financial troubles, then your meditation or prayer can end up in a state of incoherence.

Here's how heart coherence technology can help:
When you know someone is having a hard time, get into heart coherence with emWave or Inner Balance Technology, then send or radiate coherent heart care and compassion to the person or situation during your meditation or prayer. The heart energy helps them, but it also helps you stay more in balance and have less attachment to outcomes when sending care to people.

At times, a particular outcome won't always suit your personality, yet it may be spirit-directed for a higher reason in ways that we don't understand. No love and care are ever wasted; it's just that a person's own spirit decides how it wants to receive and use that care for their highest best. We have to respect the way spirit works and discerns, and be able to find more peace with its direction.

Radiating coherent heart energy can also help change the energetic environment around you. Scientific studies show that emotions not only create coherence or incoherence in our own bodies, but they radiate outward like radio waves and are detected by the nervous systems of others. In fact, the same electrical patterns that originate within our heart and synchronize our brain and body have also been shown to synchronize patterns between people and even pets.

You can learn to send or radiate coherent heart energy through a technique called the Heart Lock-In which you can use during meditation or at any time. The Heart Lock-In Technique along with the emWave or Inner Balance technology helps to empower your heart care for yourself, others and the planet. Practice of the Heart Lock-In Technique will increasingly develop your ability to sustain meditative coherence for longer periods of time.*

The Heart Lock-in® Technique

The Heart Lock-In Technique should be done for 5 minutes or longer in a quiet setting.

Step 1.
Focus your attention in the area of the heart. Imagine your breath is flowing in and out of your heart or chest area, breathing a little slower and deeper than usual.

Step 2.
Activate and sustain a regenerative feeling such as appreciation, care or compassion.

Step 3.
Radiate that renewing feeling to yourself and others.

Just radiate positive feelings from the heart in Step 3. Gently feel as if these positive feelings and heart energy are going out to others, to the world, or to yourself. If stressful thoughts or preoccupations try to take over, like thinking about the problem you are trying to help, simply bring your focus

You can also use the emWave's fun emotion visualizers to help you send heart to the planet, or play the emWave's software games that operate on your coherence level. You can save your sessions and store your data to track your progress.

and your breathing back to the area around the heart. Try to feel a place of ease in your heart, then reconnect with the feeling of care and an attitude of appreciation.

"Part of my daily centering practice has been the meditative practice of taking and sending, or Tonglen and Lojong. They are Tibetan teachings from The Path of Great Awakening. The intention with these practices is to awaken us to the openness and softness of our hearts; and in so doing, we can widen our circle of compassion. These practices, along with the HeartMath techniques, really support me each day in staying focused and in the present moment.

Recently I decided to use my emWave Desktop to see what my meditative practice would look like in the language of my heart. I opted to run the Emotion Visualizer and the feedback was immediate! It validated for me what I was feeling in my heart, great expansiveness and compassion. It was as beautiful to watch as it was to feel. The more focused I was in my practice, the more validation I received watching the screen in front of me filled with beautiful color and images. In addition, at the end of my practice I was able to look at my heart rate variability and see my progressively improving coherence scores. I love that! I now have another example of the usefulness of the emWave and can't wait to share it with clients, family, and friends."

Nellie Moore, Wellness Practitioner

Increasing Global Coherence

Today's global problems that affect us all can, at times, seem insurmountable. Many people are intuitively feeling a need to increase their heart care and kindness for others. As they free themselves from the mind's preset judgments, they begin to see that neither global nor individual peace can be realized as long as judgment, blame and separation persist between traditions and within personal relationships. People can advance in spiritual growth and effectiveness by radiating love, care and appreciation to the planet.

An important aspect of the planetary shift taking place is that heart intelligence is awakening. Many people are realizing that more heart connection is needed to enrich their own lives or to solve global problems. A momentum to become more heart-directed is building. An energetic sparkle is in the air that brings a sense of hope and adventure, yet is grounded in practicality and inspired by spirit. This increases heart intelligence and a desire for practical spirituality. It's simply a shift to heart-based living, which is not confined to religion or to any particular spiritual path. It's about taking personal responsibility for our own energy.

A new type of planetary care and service is opening up where people of all walks of life can more powerfully express their care for others and the world through collective heart-focused intention —radiating love, appreciation, care and compassion while in synchronized heart rhythm coherence.

Scientists have seen evidence of a global effect when a large number of people create similar outgoing emotional waves, whether stressful and incoherent, or positive and coherent. As people meditate for social or global coherence while on the emWave or Inner Balance technology, their hearts collectively put out an energetic wave that helps to create coherence in the environment. That energy goes out into the environment, whether the workplace, home, or society, and helps the planet. It helps to offset the incoherence and stress waves, while amplifying personal stress relief benefits at the same time.

Research has shown that 0.1 Hz (the frequency in the power spectrum at which the heart rhythm is in coherence or "in the green" on the emWave or Inner Balance technology) is the human resonant frequency—the frequency at which spirit, heart, mind, emotions and body are in alignment. The more heart coherent we are, the greater the resonant energetic connection we have with people, within ourselves and with nature. This enhances individual and collective intuitive discernment for solving personal, social, environmental and global problems.

Scientists are beginning to understand that the state of the entire natural universe is one of coherence. The implication is that all things are interconnected and communicate with one another, including nonlocally through biological and energetic fields. The Institute of HeartMath is focused on exploring and understanding this universal interconnectedness and developing internationally accessible applications to foster social, environmental and global coherence.

"Your vision will become clear only when you look into your heart ... Who looks outside, dreams. Who looks inside, awakens."

Carl Jung

The Global Coherence Initiative

The Global Coherence Initiative (GCI) is a division of the HeartMath Institute, a nonprofit research and education organization founded in 1991. A goal of GCI is to amplify individual and collective heart-focused intentions and actions for the good of humanity and our planet. The Global Coherence Initiative has the potential of unifying diverse individuals and groups across the globe through synchronized intention while in heart coherence. The energetic connectivity will enhance everyone's efforts and can lead to increased social and global harmony.

Global Coherence Initiative: https://www.heartmath.org/gci/

"The *Global Coherence Initiative is perhaps the greatest experiment in the history of the world.*"

Jack Canfield, Co-Creator of the Chicken Soup for the Soul® Series, Co-author of The Success Principles™, and founder of the Transformational Leadership Council

In Summary

The emWave or Inner Balance technology can upgrade the quality of your meditation, prayer, self-help or healing practices because it gives instant feedback when you're in and out of personal heart coherence or when your intention wobbles. Whether you are doing meditation for stress relief, for health issues, for improved focus or clarity, for manifesting affirmations or intentions, for spiritual growth, or for sending heart care to others or to the planet—you can refine and improve your effectiveness through using the emWave or Inner Balance.

The *Steps are Simple:*
Learn how to operate your emWave or Inner Balance technology.

Learn the Quick Coherence Technique. Use it with your emWave or Inner Balance technology at the start of and during your practices to build a new baseline of meditative coherence. Whether you are a beginner or a long-term meditator, you will gain more effectiveness from your meditations in shorter periods of time.

Use your emWave or Inner Balance technology with the Quick Coherence Technique to reboot and balance your system during the day. Use it to prepare for potentially challenging events and to recover quickly from stressful episodes.

Use your emWave or Inner Balance technology with the Heart Lock-In Technique to send healing heart energy to yourself, others or the planet and to help you sustain coherence for longer periods. Using emWave or Inner Balance technology in these ways will help you deal with the accelerating pace of change and stress

• • • •

levels in the world with increasing balance and more ease. Find a genuine place in the heart between focus and ease, get in heart coherence and enjoy the benefits of restored clarity and balance. Coherence is a state of renewal and creative potential in the human system, and a gateway for self-maintenance and integrating people's higher self-potentials into their human nature.

What More People are Saying about emWave and Inner Balance technology as a Meditation Assistant

"To me, the whole point of meditation is to connect me to an experience of peace, wholeness and stillness. By making the heart connection with the help of the emWave I can get there faster! When my thoughts and emotions distract me, the emWave helps me get right back on track. As I use it, I have less and less distractions and a wider, deeper, more extended experience of peace, wholeness and stillness within my mind, body and spirit."

Jasmina J. Agrillo, Stress Management Coach

"If you practice with the emWave regularly, you will find your mind in a clearer state; concentration, memory processing, and emotional stability will all improve, at least from my experience. Meditation through biofeedback is scientifically proven to achieve emotional stability and emotional calm. Nothing is perfect, but through using emWave with meditation, individuals can achieve a better balance and more coherent heart and mind rhythms. I know I do. I can honestly say that HeartMath and emWave have changed my life in such a positive way, I don't know where I'd be without it. Thank you to everyone at HeartMath."

Robert Sault, B.Sc., Medical Student

"I am a trauma survivor and with the ensuing battle with PTSD I have had great difficulty with my meditation practice. My 'fight or flight' switch is in the "on" position a lot of the time and my mind is continually hyperactive. I tried to use meditation tapes and found that I still could not stop my racing mind. I also found it hard to control the speed and depths of my breath. I recently started to use the emWave technology and found it to have a profound effect on my ability to breathe in a relaxed manner by following the breath pacer, which resulted in a less active mind. It enables me to meditate. I now use emWave several times a day, sometimes to just check in with myself and other times to relieve stress and anxiety. I am

writing a book and when I get stuck in writing, I find using emWave to be a real creativity enhancer."

Ute Lawrence, author of *The Power of Trauma: From the darkness of despair to a life filled with light* and CEO/Founder, Post Traumatic Stress Disorder Association Inc.

"I have been a meditator for 35 years and I have found heart rate variability feedback also a good way to refine my breathing. I have used HeartMath techniques and the emWave technology with several hundred people in my clinical practice as a psychologist with great success."

Dr. Gordon Davidson, Workplace Wellness Consulting

"The emWave is a great tool for me in two different types of meditations that I do and has been eye-opening for me when I am not meditating as well. When I meditate in 'normal' meditation I find that I am able to go much deeper than before. It allows me to go to the source of all Light within. It's very calming and I believe that this will enable the meditator to manifest many things. A monkey mind thought does not escape the emWave. Sometimes I may start feeling a bit cocky over the reward beeping only to instantly have it end. This is very humbling. Also now, when I'm not meditating and using the emWave, I may have a thought that is less than loving and immediately recognize that and shift. Good training! With heartfelt gratitude."

Steve Setera, Ph.D., Developing the Mind and International Crisis Relief—Community Development

"I have always known that I'm hypersensitive to other people's emotions and vibes, but I have never been able to cope with it. I have struggled with it for as long as I can remember. My emotional state fluctuates as the external 'flow' varies. The first time that I connected with emWave

Desktop, I could not believe my eyes. I immediately recognized the revelation of the heart rhythm display. I could see in real-time on the graph what I felt and I was able stop the uncontrolled oscillation. I have been working with my heart for 3 weeks now and my life has been improving. I'm gaining more and more control over my emotions and I'm learning how to deal with the invisible emotions of my wife, parents, friends and colleagues. By this recognition I'm able stay connected with my heart and help others to ease down rather than getting upset, tired or depressed. Thank you for this.

After a week I started to feel a shift in consciousness. I started to learn how the heart works: How it needs to shift from gear to gear in order to maintain its rhythm. How once the heart is in a certain state of coherence, it can absorb external spikes because it operates on automatic gear. How it can stay in a too low or too high gear when the current internal and external conditions need another rhythm and how painful it can be when there is no connection between my consciousness and my heart. I also learned that everything in the universe has a rhythm. Once you connect to it, your heart picks it up and you are not only in a state of coherent heart, but also in a coherent state of presence. I recorded 20 minutes of my data from emWave Desktop which shows an almost perfect coherent rhythm. I called it peace."

Frans van der Pluijm, Chemical Engineer

"I will never forget how I felt during and after my first meditation retreat. Day one. Twelve hours sitting still. In silence. Argh. Impossible. My brain would not shut up: What's for lunch? How long before lunch? What smells so bad? What's for dinner? After another twelve hours sitting still. A shift. An oasis. A respite from chaos. And at the end? WOW!! Everything was so vibrant and bright! And calm and peaceful at the same time. I felt like I had come home for the first time. I was hooked. Quite literally. And that became a problem.

Every weekend I would go back and have to sit through a day of pain unwinding the week's stress before I felt good again. Then I had to meditate for longer and longer periods of time in order to experience that 'shine. ' By year five of my meditative journey, I was leaving regular life to meditate on silent retreats for months at a time. I was getting up earlier and earlier every day because I felt that I 'needed' more and more meditation to face the world. Some days I was up at 4:00 a.m. to be able to meditate for four or five hours. Other days I would miss classes in college, or pass on fun activities with my friends, if I felt something was taking me away from meditation and that 'peaceful' zone. It was compromising my relationships and time for work and school.

Then, I found the emWave technology and I was like, 'WHAT??' With the emWave, I could get into the 'zone' that it took me hours to achieve in meditation in a matter of minutes! Instantly quiet mind, instant peace. Not only that, but the technology helps me carry the meditative zone into my life, so I no longer have to leave life to enter a state of peace. The two go hand in hand. This has been miraculous for my relationships and given me much more time for work and play. Now, when I do have the luxury to meditate for longer hours, using the emWave or Inner Balance technology at the start makes that time count for more. Instead of clocking time in a 'zoned-out' meditation to finally get to peace, the emWave or Inner Balance technology helps me get in the peace 'zone. ' Thank you for creating this user-friendly facilitation to something that's so important to me."

Sheva Carr, Doctor of Oriental Medicine

"I have only had my portable emWave for about a week. But what a week of learning it has been! As someone who both uses and teaches breathing techniques for relaxation and has worked with mindfulness meditation, it was not a difficult task to turn the light from red to green. And the physical awareness that accompanies the green light seems very close to what I experience as a Reiki practitioner when I am channeling Reiki energy. And that also seems reasonable to me. One real 'aha' moment came when I was out walking in my yard. It was a beautiful sunny fall day, quite unusual for Vermont this time of year and I was seeing if I could stay in coherence as I enjoyed the beauty around. As I walked, my thoughts wandered a bit as they are prone to do, and I realized that I was experiencing a long standing annoyance with a particular situation in my life. And no sooner had my thoughts focused on this annoyance, than the light was red. That wasn't any surprise. What surprised me was my response which was, 'So I am no longer in coherence when I think about it in that way, but those are the feelings I have always had about this situation. And I really don't want to change the way I feel.' And then, as I continued my walk, I thought about how holding onto that annoyance was really costing me at the physical level.

I had started using the emWave to help me lower my blood pressure without adding additional Pharmaceuticals to my regimen. And I was almost immediately successful in doing that. But each time I insisted on holding onto that anger (righteous as it is) and annoyance and the need to be the one who is right, I see I am introducing stresses to my body that are not really necessary. And that red light shows me bright and clear that that is where I am at the moment. Perhaps I don't need to carry that annoyance anymore. Many thanks for all of the work and research that has gone into this wonderful, simple, and yet profound tool. I am certain that I will continue to work with it and to recommend and introduce it to others."

Sylvia Newberry, Herbalist and Energy Healer

"I use the emWave a lot. I do believe that the most essential attitude in life is the capacity to be in the here and now, as conscious as possible.

HeartMath Meditation Assistant

Integrating emWave® & Inner Balance™ Technologies

● ● ● ●

Happiness can only be found in the present. Only the present gives 'the present' — the gift of happiness. Worries, desires, so many things distract me from that ability; so many things can pull me back in the past or catapult me into the future. My emWave trains me in 'present' awareness. I often think I'm meditating and then the red light heals me from that illusion and I get back on track. This biofeedback system is brilliant. If the whole world was obliged to practice with the emWave for 20 minutes a day, the world would be a better place. Global warming, terrorism, nuclear threats are not the priority. The priority is people who are connected to their heart and soul, and by doing so they connect automatically to God, their higher self, guide, angel, conscience, or whatever name they give to the transcending reality. The emWave or Inner Balance technology helps us to find that purity. Because of its proofing quality, the emWave's green, blue and red light, confronts us with a reality which cannot be denied. In a world where many are lost, it is a sign of hope."

Lutgart Naudts, Psychiatric Nurse

"I use my emWave every day. I start off using it first thing in the morning before and after my Heart Lock-In practice. At first I was only using it after, but, oh man, does it make for a much better heart focus and Heart Lock-In when using it before and after. I keep the emWave close to my computer and as the day goes on and more pressure is felt, I use it. It helps remind me to breathe and stay in my heart. I also pick it up when I'm not feeling any pressure, just to see if I am as balanced as I think I am. It keeps me honest. Years of meditation haven't ever given me the instant results that I get with the emWave. Although I do still love to meditate, when I do so now, I relax much easier and get to where I want to be much quicker. It's fun to see how fast I can get to green. It has actually

become a game I play with myself. Thank you, thank you, thank you for this phenomenal tool."

Lynn Bolaza, CFO, Heart of Health, Inc.

"I believe using the emWave has helped me reach a stage of development that I could not have reached without that real time feedback. I have done a lot of meditating and participated in a lot of talking and listening self-development processes during the last 40 years, and I think I plateaued out in my development. The HeartMath information, and especially the emWave, have helped me open into a new phase of development which seems to be accelerating. The emwave is helping me make distinctions and discernments about my inner states that I was unaware of. So I'm very grateful for it and want to make maximum use of it and contribute to it in any what that I can."

Sanford Anderson, Social Entrepreneur

"Teaching you how to achieve self-regulation is the mission of Inner Balance.. It's a trainer, showing you how to calm yourself, relieving stress and giving you more control over your emotions. The goal is to achieve the app's green color of total relaxation — or as HeartMath calls it, "coherence." As I settled in, the software indicated that my "heart, mind and emotions were in sync." It felt that way, too."... You could practice these techniques yourself, without an iPhone, iPad or iPod touch and this little earlobe clip. However, if you aren't sure how to make that happen, this Inner Balance hardware and its free software can show you precisely what kinds of thoughts and actions actually work, and how to achieve coherence. I think if you practice with this system three times a day as its makers recommend, it could change your life."

Charlie White, technology reviewer for Mashable.com http://mashable. com/2013/03/03/inner-balance/

● ● ● ●

Notes

Other Resources

HeartMath's Heart Rate Variability (HRV) technology is a scientifically validated system that trains you into an optimal high performance state in which the heart, brain and nervous system are operating in sync and in balance. We call this state coherence. HeartMath's HRV products measure your coherence level, store your data and connect you to the HeartCloud™ for community support and rewards. As you increase your coherence level, your ability to focus and take charge of emotional reactions improves and you have greater access to your heart's intuitive guidance system for making effective choices.

The emWave2® or Inner Balance™

Portable and convenient ways to reduce stress, balance your emotions, increase your cognitive functions and enhance performance. Used just a few minutes a day, this simple-to-use technology helps to transform anger, anxiety or frustration into inner peace, ease and mental clarity. Health, communication and relationships improve.

emWave Pro for PC & Mac

Using a pulse sensor plugged into a USB port, emWave Pro collects and translates HRV (heart rate variability) coherence data into user-friendly graphics. It provides a Coherence Coach®, fun visualizers and games that respond to your coherence level. emWave Pro and emWave Pro Plus are multiuser and ideal for classrooms and for health professionals to keep track of client data and progress.

www.heartmath.com or call 1 -800-450-9111

Training and Certification Programs

Add Heart® Daily Calls
Dial in or log in to join a 10 minute call with a HeartMath staff trainer to increase your mental and emotional fitness and practice the Heart Lock-In® Technique together.

Become an Add Heart® Facilitator
Become an approved facilitator to learn and share with others some of the science that underpins the HeartMath system, an effective three-step technique for getting into coherence, and how to use the Inner Balance Trainer. In this online course, you learn how to share what you are learning in personal and professional situations.

Become a HeartMath® Certified Coach/Mentor
Learn via an 8 week telephone course HeartMath's scientifically–validated tool set and how to teach these tools to clients. HeartMath Coach/Mentors are licensed to teach the HeartMath System in a one-on-one setting.

Become a HeartMath® Certified Trainer
Attend a full immersion 4.5 day certification program. HeartMath Certified Trainers are licensed to provide HeartMath workshops in a 6 hour program, and in shorter modules, or to embed HeartMath modules, techniques, tools and scientific concepts into other training programs.

Become a HeartMath® Certified Practitioner
The HeartMath Interventions Certification Program is for health professionals who want to add HeartMath techniques and technology to their practice to improve patient and client outcomes. The program includes live and recorded webinars, video presentations and home study.

HeartMath Institute
HeartMath Institute (HMI) is nonprofit organization that researches and develops scientifically based tools to help people bridge the connection between their hearts and minds. It also provides HeartMath programs to social service agencies, and curricula for children and schools pre K-college. **www.heartmath.org.**

HeartMath LLC
HeartMath LLC is a cutting-edge health and performance company that provides a range of unique services, products, and technology to improve well-being, while dramatically reducing stress and overwhelm and boosting performance and productivity. **www.heartmath.com.**

Call 1 -800-450-9111 or visit www.heartmath.com

HeartMath Meditation Assistant

Integrating emWave® & Inner Balance™ Technologies

●●●●

Heart Intelligence: Connecting with the Intuitive Guidance of the Heart

By Doc Childre, Howard Martin, Deborah Rozman Ph.D. and Rollin McCraty Ph.D.

Our newest book, Heart Intelligence, provides breakthrough research linking the physical heart to the spiritual (energetic) heart. This book provides simple techniques for accessing our heart's intuitive intelligence for moment–to–moment guidance and discernment

Transforming Depression: The HeartMath® Solution to Feeling Overwhelmed, Sad, and Stressed

by Doc Childre and Deborah Rozman, Ph.D.

Transforming Anxiety: The HeartMath Solution for Overcoming Fear and Worry and Creating Serenity

by Doc Childre and Deborah Rozman, Ph.D.

Transforming Stress: The HeartMath Solution For Relieving Worry, Fatigue, and Tension

by Doc Childre and Deborah Rozman, Ph.D.

Transforming Anger, The HeartMath Solution for Letting Go of Rage, Frustration and Irritation

by Doc Childre and Deborah Rozman, Ph.D.

The HeartMath Solution

by Doc Childre and Howard Martin

www.heartmath.com or call 1-800-450-9111

HeartMath is a registered trademark of Quantum Intech, Inc. For all HeartMath trademarks go to www.heartmath.com/trademarks

Printed in Great Britain
by Amazon

18327123R00041